Fast and Fun Ways to Read Body Language

Proven Tips, Tools and Tactics to Non-Verbal Communication

Divya Parekh

ii

Special Invitation

Visioning and Goal Charting to Success

SUCCESS is yours with the right VISION and GOALS. With this report: develop unique vision; think strategically over the long term; take small, measurable action steps that guide you to your vision, eliminate distractions and be focused on your purpose

Visioning and Goal Charting to Success

http://www.divyaparekh.com/product/visioning-and-goal-charting-knowing-the-dream-living-the-expedition-and-reaching-the-destination/

Or

http://bit.ly/1iV4Blj

$50.00 value DISC (Personality Style) and Hidden Motivators Assessment - COMPLIMENTARY FOR THE READERS ONLY

Achieve PRODUCTIVITY, PERSONAL and FINANCIAL SUCCESS in your life by: Understanding yourself. You are invited to take a complimentary Hidden Motivators Profile assessment (invitation code: 44voyage) because understanding yourself will help you maximize PRODUCTIVITY, PERSONAL and FINANCIAL SUCCESS when your MOTIVATORS are at work.

http://dpgroup.abeo.us/voyage/

Table of Contents

Preface

The human body is the best picture of the human soul.

Ludwig Wittgenstein

Preface

Can you tell if someone is telling the truth just by looking at them? It is a skill that a lot of people do not have. Through Body Language Basics you will be given a set of tools to use to your advantage. These tools can be utilized in the office and at home. Understanding Body Language will provide you a great advantage in your daily communications.

Body Language Basics will provide you with a great set of skills to understand that what is not said is just as important as what is said. It will also give you the ability to see and understand how your own Body Language is being seen. You will be able to adjust and improve the way you communicate through non-verbal communications.

Chapter One:
Communicating with Body Language

The body never lies.
Martha Graham

We are constantly communicating, even when we are not speaking. Unspoken communication makes up over half of what we tell others and they tell us. It affects our work and personal relationships. Improves negotiating, management, and interpersonal skills by correctly interpreting body language and important signals.

Learning a New Language

In many ways understanding body language is like learning a foreign language. There are a few tips that make learning any language, even a nonverbal one, easier.

Tips:

- Set Goals: Make sure that your goals are realistic and have specific timelines.

- Devote time to learning: Schedule time to practice. Do not rely on spare time.

- Practice daily: Hone skills by continued practice.

- Enjoy the process: You are not in school. Relax and have fun with your new skill.

The Power of Body Language

Understanding body language does more than improve relationships. You will get insight into the thoughts and feelings of those around you. Because it is not a conscious form of communication, people betray themselves in their body language. Body language is powerful in several ways.

Power of Body Language:

- It is honest: Body language conveys truth, even when words do not.

- Creates self-awareness: Understanding body language helps you identify your own actions that hinder success.

- Understand feelings: Body language shows feelings and motive such as aggression, submission, deception, etc. Use these as cues to your communication.

- Enhance listening and communication skills: Paying attention to body language makes someone a better listener. Hear between the words spoken to what is being said.

More than Words

Much of the way people communicate is nonverbal. Body language specifically focuses on physical, not tone, or pitch. It includes the following characteristics:

Body Language:

- Proximity: The distance between people

- Positioning: Position of a body

- Facial expression: The eyes are particularly noticed.

- Touching: This includes objects, people, and themselves.

- Breathing: The rate of respiration is telling.

Actions Speak Louder than Words

Our impressions of each other are based on more than words. People can have cordial conversations and not like each other. The actions that we take are stronger than our words. For example, a person may dismiss someone using body language and not say anything negative. Like it or not, our body language makes a lasting impression on the people around us.

What Actions Can Say:

- Deception

- Confidence

- Nerves

- Boredom

- Emotions

- Attraction

- Being open

- Being closed off

Please note that this is not a thorough list of what body language can communicate, a complete list would take many pages.

Practical Illustration

Jim had to hire a new personal assistant. He needed someone organized and personable. Jen answered all of the interview questions perfectly. She had the necessary training and education, so Jim hired her. After a few weeks, some of Jim's coworkers complained about her behavior. They accused her of being aggressive and insubordinate, but she never said anything specifically rude or hostile. Her tone and body language, however, were extremely aggressive. For example, she rolled her eyes when people asked her questions. Jim had to coach Jen on her nonverbal communication, and going forward he added a body language evaluation to his interview process.

Chapter Two:
Reading Body Language

Emotion always has its roots in the
unconscious and manifests itself in the body.
Irene Claremont de Castillejo

We are constantly reading the body language of others, even when we are not aware of it. Actively reading body language, however, will provide valuable insight and improve communication. Pay attention to the positions and movements of people around you. Specifically their head positions, physical gestures, and eyes.

Head Position

The head is an obvious indicator of feelings and thoughts. The position of the head speaks volumes, making it the perfect place to start. While it takes practice to accurately interpret head position, the basic positions, and movements that are not extremely difficult to identify.

Movement and Position:

- **Nodding:** Nodding typically indicates agreement. The speed of the nod, however, indicates different things. A slow nod can be a sign of interest or a polite, fake signal. Look to other eyes for confirmation. A fast nod signals impatience with the speaker.

- **Head up:** This position indicates that the person is listening without bias.

- **Head down:** This position indicates disinterest or rejection for what is said. When done during an activity, it signals weakness or tiredness.

- **Tilted to the side:** This means a person is thoughtful or vulnerable. It can signal trust.

- **Head high:** Holding the head high signals confidence or feelings of superiority.

- **Chin up:** The chin up indicates defiance or confidence.

- **Head forward:** Facing someone directly indicates interest. It is a positive signal.

- **Tilted down:** Tilting the head down signals disapproval.

- **Shaking:** A shaking head indicates disagreement. The faster the shaking, the stronger the disagreement.

Translating Gestures into Words

Scientific studies show that the part of the human brain that comprehends words is the same part of the brain that comprehends gestures. Gestures are also called movement clusters because it is more than a body position. We use gestures when we speak, typically hand gestures. They enhance meaning, or can be used by themselves.

Translations:

- **Pointing finger**: This is an aggressive movement. When a wink is added, however, it is a positive confirmation of an individual.

- **Finger moves side to side**: This motion acts as a warning to stop something.

- **Finger moves up and down**: This acts as a reprimand or places emphasis on what is said.

- **Thumbs up**: Thumbs up is a sign of approval.

- **Thumbs down**: This is a sign of disapproval.

- **Touch index finger to thumb**: The sign indicates OK.

Open Vs. Closed Body Language

Body language is often defined as open or closed. Being open or closed has many different causes. Open body language can come from passivity, aggression, acceptance, supplication, or relaxation. Closed body language may be caused by the desire to hide, self-protection, cold, or relaxation.

Closed body language:

- **Arms crossed:** This stance is often defensive or hostile.

- **Legs crossed when seated:** Cross legs can indicate caution. One leg over the other at the knee may indicate stubbornness.

- **Arm or object in front of the body:** This can coincide with nervousness and is a form of self-protection.

- **Legs crossed when standing:** This may mean someone is insecure when combined with crossed arms. By itself, it can signal interest.

Open body language:

- **Legs not crossed:** This is an open, relaxed position.

- **Arms not crossed:** Open arms indicate openness; although the hands may indicate aggression, supplication, or insecurity, depending on their position.

The Eyes Have It

People give a great deal away through their eyes. The eyes are an important factor when reading a person's body language. When combined with body position, the eyes will provide a more accurate translation of body language.

Looks:

- **Looking to the left**: Eyes in this direction can mean someone is remembering something. Combined with a downward look, it indicates the self-communication. When looking up, it means facts are being recalled.

- **Sideways**: Looking sideways means someone is conjuring sounds. Right, is associated with imagination, and may mean a story. Left is accessing memory.

- **Looking to the right**: Looks to the right indicates imagination. It can mean guessing or lying. Combined with looking down, it means there is a self-question. Combined with looking up, it can mean lying.

- **Direct eye contact**: When speaking, this means sincerity and honesty. When listening, it indicates interest.

- **Wide eyes**: Widening eyes signal interest.

- **Rolled eyes**: Rolled eyes mean frustration. They can be considered a sign of hostility.

- **Blinking:** Frequent blinking indicates excitement. Infrequent blinking signals a boredom or concentration, depending focus.

- **Winking:** A wink is a friendly gesture or secret joke.

- **Rubbing eyes:** Rubbing eyes may be caused by tiredness. It can also indicate disbelief or being disturbed.

Practical Illustration

Mark is a sales executive who led a meeting hoping to reach new clients and increase his sales. He thought the presentation went well. Many people attending began to nod vigorously. He took this as a sign of agreement and added a few more facts to cement his position, which lengthened the presentation a few minutes. After the presentation, however, only two attendees chose to sign up. Most made comments about being late and promised to meet with him later.

Chapter Three:
Body Language Mistakes

The biggest single problem in communication
is the illusion it is taking place.
George Bernard Shaw

There are different factors that will create false body language signals. This is why it is so important to examine the positions and gestures as a whole when attempting to interpret body language. To prevent body language mistakes, become aware of these factors and think carefully when reading body language.

Poor Posture

Posture can lead to unfair judgments and prejudices. Often, poor posture is seen as a closed body language that people assume is caused by a lack of confidence. There are, however, many different reasons why someone can have poor posture. While it is true that most people can improve on their posture, the changes that can be made to a person's musculoskeletal structure are limited. Always pay attention to other cues, and do not make rash judgments based solely on posture.

Some Causes of Poor Posture:

- **Injury**: Both acute injuries and repetitive motion injuries can alter someone's posture.

- **Illness**: Autoimmune diseases, such as arthritis, can damage the skeletal structure.

- **Skeletal structure**: Scoliosis and other problems with the spine will affect posture.

- **Temperature**: People may take a closed posture when they are cold.

Invading Personal Space

Invading personal space is seen as an act of hostility. Western societies typically use five different zones, depending on the social situations.

1. **12 feet**: This zone is for the public. The purpose is to avoid physical interaction.

2. **4 feet:** This zone is reserved for social interactions such as business settings. Touching requires the individual to move forward.

3. **18 inches:** This is a personal zone. It allows contact, and it is reserved for friends and family.

4. **6 inches:** This zone is reserved for close relationships. This zone can be invaded in crowds or sports.

5. **0 to 6 inches:** This zone is reserved for intimate relationships.

It is essential to remember that these zones are part of most Western cultures. There are reasons why people will invade personal space that have nothing to do with hostility.

Personal Space Differences:

- **Culture**: Each culture has different boundaries and personal space.

- **Background**: Personal history and background will affect an individual's concept of personal space.

- **Activity**: Some activities require people to work closely. This should be considered before assuming someone is invading personal space.

Quick Movements

Quick movements may be interpreted as a sign of nervousness. They may, however, be used to draw attention to specific information when speaking. Consistent jerking movements, however, do not always indicate nerves or negative emotions. Do not make a snap judgment about quick movements. There are reasons why movements may seem quick or jerking.

May alter movement:

- Stress
- Illness
- Exhaustion
- Cold

Fidgeting

Most people fidget from time to time. In interviews and social settings, fidgeting can indicate nervousness, boredom, frustration, stress, or self-consciousness. It is an outlet to release feelings or an attempt at self-comfort. Besides emotions, there are a number of other reasons why people may fidget.

Other Reasons for Fidgeting:

- Attention deficit disorder: ADD and ADHD are often accompanied by fidgeting.

- Hormone imbalances: These may be accompanied by nervous energy.

- Blood sugar imbalances: Fidgeting accompanies sugar highs.

- Imbalanced brain chemistry: These may increase tension.

- Medications: Steroids and other medications can cause imbalances

Practical Illustration

Sara was not impressed with Jon when she first saw him. His shoulders were hunched over in a closed off position. She went into the interview knowing that it would be a waste of her time. Jon's head position, however, showed interest. He had an engaging smile and was genuinely interested in the position. Given his skills and complete body language assessment, Sara became more positive about Jon as a candidate. The interview revealed that Jon had worked a manufacturing job where his upper back was injured.

Chapter Four:
Gender Differences

*A blur of blinks, taps, jiggles, pivots and shifts ... the body
language of a man wishing urgently to be elsewhere.*
Edward R. Murrow

Not all body language is universal. There are differences in the
way that men and women communicate. Body language is often
confused between genders. In order to prevent
miscommunications, it is important to understand the signals
that are common to most people as well as the different signals
that men and women communicate with their body language.

Facial Expressions

Men and women share the universal facial expressions, but
there are some differences in use and perception. For example,
women typically tend to smile more often than men. Women
frequently smile to be polite or fulfill cultural expectations. The
meanings behind smiles are often misinterpreted. Additionally,
people judge the same facial expressions on men and women
differently. Women, for example, were thought to be angrier
and less happy than men, according to a study published by the
American Psychological Association, even though they all had
the same facial expressions.

Personal Distances

Personal space and personal distance change with each individual. Everyone has his or her own idea of personal distance, which is the comfortable distance that someone wishes to keep from another person. Gender, however, often affects one's sense of personal distance.

Men: Men generally take more space than women, and they employ larger personal distances. Men are less likely to stand close to each other, even when they are all friends. Additionally, they create larger buffer zones using items such as coats, cups, papers, etc. Men usually expect their buffer zones to be respected and do not respond well to someone invading their personal space.

Women: Women generally employ smaller personal distances with each other or with male friends. They tend to increase personal distance with strange men. Women also create buffer zones, but they are typically smaller than male buffer zones. Women are more likely to draw back when their zones are invaded, and female buffer zones are not always respected. People are more likely to move a woman's purse than a man's coat.

Female Body Language

There are some subtle differences to note when interpreting female body language. Culture plays a role in what is considered appropriate body language. Female body language changes over time, and it is not universal to all women. There are, however, some basic actions that many women have in common.

Body Language:

- **Body Position and posture:** Many women use closed body language. This may stem from a cultural convention to appear smaller. Women, however, will straighten their posture to look more attractive.

- **Leaning:** Women will lean forward when they are interested in something or someone. They lean away when displeased or uncomfortable.

- **Smiling:** We have already mentioned that women are more likely to smile. While it is often a friendly gesture, it is a probably a polite gesture when the eyes are not engaged.

- **Eye contact:** Eye contact indicates interest (either in what is said or the individual). Dilated pupils are another sign of interest.

- **Mirroring:** Women often mirror, or copy, the actions of each other. They will only occasionally mirror men.

- **Legs and feet:** The legs and feet typically point in the direction of a woman's interest. This includes romantic interest.

- **Touching:** Women are more likely to touch each other than men are.

- **Tapping:** Tapping or fidgeting is a sign that a woman is annoyed or uncomfortable.

Male Body Language

Male body language is not universal to all men. There are, however, certain aspects of body language that are common to many men. Male body language is often seen as more aggressive and dominating. Women are sometimes encouraged to adapt male body language in the workplace.

Body Language:

- **Stance:** Men often choose wide stances to increase their size. Spread legs and a straight back, both sitting and standing, indicates confidence. Closed body language does not.

- **Eye contact:** Men will make eye contact, but eye contact can be seen as a dominating or hostile act when it lasts too long. Occasional eye aversion is normal. Like women, pupils dilate with interest.

- **Mirroring:** Men do not typically mirror each other. They often mirror women to show their interest.

- **Legs and feet:** Like women, the legs and feet typically point in the direction of a man's interest. This includes romantic interest.

- **Smiling**: Men do not smile as often as women in social settings; their facial expressions are often reserved. They do, however, occasionally use forced smiles. Men often smile when happy or to engage someone's interest.

- **Hands**: Men are more likely to fidget than women. This is not necessarily a sign of insecurity or boredom, just a way to use energy.

Practical Illustration

Tom was attracted to his coworker Lisa. Lisa always smiled when she saw him come in. She even laughed at his jokes. Tom would spend time in her cubicle, and she never told him to leave. She simply continued working, leaning toward her computer while he talked to her back. Tom was certain that Lisa would go out with him, and one day he asked her. To his surprise, Lisa was annoyed by his request. She told him that she did nothing to encourage his attention and that she would file a harassment report if he asked her out again.

Chapter Five:
Nonverbal Communication

What you do speaks so loud that I cannot hear what you say.
Ralph Waldo Emmerson

We all communicate nonverbally. The image that we project from our nonverbal communication affects the way that our spoken communication is received. While interpreting body language is important, it is equally important to understand what your nonverbal communication is telling others. It takes more than words to persuade others.

Common Gestures

Many gestures that we make are unconscious movements or mannerisms. Being aware of what our gestures mean will make us aware of what we are communicating. The following list is not comprehensive, but it is a good place to start.

Unconscious Gestures:

- **Biting nails**: This may mean insecurity or nerves.

- **Turning away:** Looking away indicates that you do not believe someone.

- **Pulling ears:** Tugging at ears can indicate indecision.

- **Head tilt:** A brief head tilt means interest. Holding a tilt equals boredom.

- **Open palms:** Showing palms is a sign of innocence or sincerity.

- **Rubbing hands together**: Rubbing hands together is a sign of excitement or anticipation.

- **Touching the chin:** This signals that a decision is being made.

- **Hand on the cheek:** Touching the cheek indicates someone is thinking.

- **Drumming fingers:** This is a sign of impatience.

- **Touching the nose:** People often associate touching the nose with lying. It can also signal doubt or rejection.

The Signals You Send to Others

You are always sending signals to other people. These signals come through body language, voice, appearance, and personal distance.

- **Body language**: Body language includes posture, gestures, and facial expressions.

- **Appearance**: A person's hygiene and dress send signals to others. People make negative assumptions based on a disheveled appearance.

- **Personal distance**: Too great a personal distance makes people appear cold. On the other hand, not respecting the personal distance of others will have negative consequences.

- **Voice**: Tone is important to the way we communicate. Emotions are conveyed through tone.

It's Not What You Say, it's How You Say It

Miscommunication is a common problem in personal and business relationships. Paying attention to the way that you communicate will help prevent any miscommunications. You must take note of the tone, pitch, and timbre of your voice.

- **Pitch:** People tend to naturally respect deeper voices. High-pitched voices are viewed as a sign of immaturity. Try a lower, even pitch. Even a neutral tone can make a person appear weak or insecure when there is a higher pitch at the end of a statement, like questions have.

- **Speed:** Keep a moderate pace. Speaking too quickly will cause confusion, and speaking too slowing will make it difficult to keep attention.

- **Loudness**: Speak up; quiet voices can be viewed as submissive. Be careful, however, not to accidentally yell.

- **Tone**: Tone conveys emotion, so avoid sarcasm and condescension. Vary your tone to prevent boring listeners with a monotone presentation.

What Your Posture Says

Posture is the basis of body language communication. People respond well to good posture, and having good posture improves physical and emotional health. Slouching is seen as a sign of insecurity or weakness. Confident body language demands good posture.

Posture Communication:

- **Standing or sitting erect**: Standing straight communicates confidence. It will also prevent musculoskeletal pain.

- **Hunching over**: This is closed body language and can signal unhappiness or insecurity.

- **Ducking or shrugging the head**: This is a protective or submissive move to appear smaller. It is not equated with confidence.

Correct Posture:

- **Stand and sit straight:** Straight posture maintains the natural curve of the spine. This is achieved by pulling in the abdominal muscles, pushing the shoulders back, and lifting the chest.

- **Head position:** Hold the head upright and look to the front. This will protect the natural shape of the neck.

- **Relaxation:** Posture should not be forced or stiff. Someone with straight posture should look and feel relaxed.

Practical Illustration

A supervisor of Nutime Production consistently has low employee evaluations. Employees felt that he was rude and authoritative. The supervisor attempted to be more careful in his choice of words, and he scheduled an assessment to point out his problem. The assessment showed that the supervisor's tone often conveyed condescension and sarcasm. Additionally, his body language and gestures indicated impatience and aggression. His nonverbal communication was stronger than his words. The supervisor was assigned a communications course.

Chapter Six:
Facial Expressions

Beauty without expression is boring.
Ralph Waldo Emerson

Facial expressions are an important part of body language. We use our faces to express ourselves, and we all interpret the facial expressions we see. While some facial expressions are cultural, some facial expressions are universal. Understanding the basics of facial expressions and decoding them will help you determine what people are feeling and facilitate better communication.

Linked with Emotion

Many scientists agree that facial expressions are linked to emotions. Different feelings create physical responses within the body, and facial expressions are emotional responses to situations. Because of the emotional connection, it is not easy to continually fake facial expressions. A flash of true emotion will typically flicker across the face, even when feelings are kept in check. Not only are emotions shown with facial expressions; the degree of emotion a person feels is visible on the face. For example, you can see the difference between a face that shows sadness and one that shows sorrow.

Micro-Expressions

We all hide negative or unwanted emotions from time to time. We can even mask our facial expressions to fit social situations. Feelings can occasionally slip out in the form of micro-expressions. These brief, involuntary expressions betray emotions, and they typically last 1/25 of a second. For example, someone gives a brief sneer but smiles when running into an acquaintance. Most people do not consciously notice micro-expressions. In fact, roughly ten percent of people will knowingly pick up on the micro-expressions of others.

Most micro-expressions are based on universal facial expressions. Being aware of these facial expressions will make micro expressions easier to catch. Noticing micro-expressions can help determine if someone is lying. It is not foolproof, however. For example, someone can be afraid of being caught in a lie or of not being believed.

Facial Action Coding System (FACS)

The Facial Action Coding System (FACS) is a complex system attributed to Dr. Paul Ekman. This system breaks down the muscle movements of micro-expressions into numbered action units (AUs). The muscles that relax or contract with emotion are identified to show the feeling behind each movement of the face. There are AUs identified in the upper and lower face. The meanings behind these involuntary muscle movements are interpreted by the FACS system. The intensity, duration, and asymmetry of expressions are also noted.

Upper Face:

- Eyebrows
- Forehead
- Eyelids

Lower Face:

- Up/Down
- Horizontal
- Oblique
- Orbital
- Miscellaneous

Example:

- An insincere smile will only trigger the zygomatic major muscle. A sincere smile will also include the lower part of the orbicularis oculi.

Universal Facial Expressions

Many facial expressions are learned from one's family and culture. There are, however, facial expressions that all people are believed to share in common. These are the universal facial expressions. Success with FACS and interpreting micro-expressions requires an understanding of universal facial expressions. There are different lists of universal facial expressions, but most lists include the same six expressions.

Facial Expressions:

- **Happiness**: More than a smile is needed to indicate happiness. Genuine happiness should include the eyes. Eyelids crinkle and crow's feet become visible.

- **Anger**: A frown typically accompanies anger. Additionally, the eyes narrow, the chin points forward, and the eyebrows furrow.

- **Fear**: Wide eyes and slightly raised eyebrows signal fear. The lips may be parted or stretched when the mouth is closed.

- **Surprise:** Surprise is similar to fear. The eyebrows fully raise and the eyes are wide with surprise. The mouth, however, is usually open.

- **Sadness:** The mouth turns down when someone is sad. A crease in the forehead and quivering chin accompany this slight frown.

- **Disgust:** The expression of disgust includes the nose. The nose wrinkles, the lips part, and the eyes narrow.

Note: Contempt is not always a universally recognized facial expression. It is useful to recognize, however, and includes a sneer with the side of the mouth elevated.

Practical Illustration

Jane attended a FACS class to improve hers sales. After the class, she began to close sales quickly. Her sales increased by 20 percent after the first quarter. Jane learned to stop spending time with potential clients who showed contempt and disgust. The skills helped her identify what made clients happy and address potentially difficult situations before anger boiled over. Due to her results, her department invested in further FACS training.

Chapter Seven:
Body Language in Business

The more elaborate our means of communication,
the less we communicate.
Joseph Priestly

Body language can provide people in business with a key advantage. Learn how to adjust your body language to each situation, as you identify the needs, thoughts, and feelings of those you do business with every day. A basic understanding of body language will strengthen negotiating strategies and other business tactics.

Communicate with Power

Powerful communication breeds confidence and respect. It is important that people sense power without aggression. Communicating with power requires practice, but it is an effective business tool.

Powerful Movements:

- **Stance**: A wide stance with the feet apart indicates power. Hands on the hips with the elbows out take up more space and also indicates power.

- **Positioning**: Avoid open space at your back. It is known to elevate stress. Open spaces can be used to make others more vulnerable.

- **Walk**: Walk quickly and take long strides. Be careful not to run, and keep the back and neck erect.

- **Handshake**: Offer a firm handshake, and keep the hand vertical. Placing the palm up because it is a submissive gesture. The palm down is a dominating gesture.

- **Sitting**: Sit with the legs slightly apart. Another powerful pose is sitting with one leg crossed over the other and hands behind the head. Be careful, however, because this position makes many women uncomfortable.

Cultural Differences

International business means working with different cultural backgrounds. While certain expressions are universally recognized, many gestures are cultural. It is essential to research the etiquette and communication style of any culture you do business with ahead of time.

Examples of Differences:

- **Feet**: Pointing feet at people or showing the soles of the feet is disrespectful in many Middle East and Asian cultures.

- **Eye contact**: Different cultures view prolonged eye contact as disrespectful.

- **Hand gestures**: Avoid Western hand gestures when communicating with people from different cultures. Many of them, such as thumbs up, are rude.

- **Head**: Individuals from certain parts of India may move their heads to the side when they agree.

Building Trust

Monitor body language to build trust with business partners. Personal perception builds trust. There are steps that anyone can take to create a rapport of trust.

Steps:

- **Remove barriers:** Physical barriers create a defensive line and do not increase trust.

- **Smile:** A genuine smile helps build trust. People can typically pick up on fake smiles, and insincerity does not engender trust.

- **Body position:** Remain relaxed to build trust.

- **Listen:** Active listening and repeating information helps connect with people.

Mirroring

Mirroring helps build rapport. Mirroring occurs when we copy the movements and gestures of others to show similarities. The perception that people are similar creates trust. Typically mirroring comes easier to women. Women will mirror each other in social settings. Men usually mirror women in romantic situations. In the business setting, consciously mirroring a client or colleague will have dramatic results.

What to Mirror:

- **Smile**: Smile when the client does.

- **Height:** Some people mirror height by stooping or stretching their bodies.

- **Gestures:** Copy the gestures used.

- **Speech:** Monitor the tone, pitch, and rhythm the individual uses.

- **Breathe:** Matching breathing rates will help create a bond.

Practical Illustration

William was in charge of international accounts. He was sure that his ability to read body language would give him an advantage. The company was expanding into Asian markets. At his first meeting, William focused on his body language. He gave the associate his full attention, even pointing his body and feet at the direction of the associate. The meeting did not go as well as expected, and his associate seemed uncomfortable. William researched the cultural conventions of his associate and learned that he was being insulting with his feet. The subsequent meetings were much more effective.

Chapter Eight:
Lying and Body Language

You can tell a lot by someone's body language.
Harvey Wolter

Body language can expose deception. Close observation of body language can indicate that someone is hiding something. Be careful about interpreting every action as a lie. A number of factors, including stress and insecurity, will cause suspicious body language. When there are multiple indications of deception in a person's body language, however, further investigation may be warranted.

Watch Their Hands

We all communicate with our hands. We can even communicate deception without knowing what we are doing. Several movements can indicate someone is hiding something.

Hands:

- **Palms down:** Showing your palms is a sign of sincerity. Keeping the palms down signals that someone is hiding something.

- **Self-touching**: Self-touching may be a calming action, but be alert when someone touches this or her face. Hands at the nose and mouth are often seen as an attempt to hide the spoken lie.

- **Hidden hands**: Hand gestures are a natural part of communication. Many people will suddenly hide their hands when telling lies. Lack of hand movement may also indicate lying.

Forced Smiles

We have already mentioned smiling. A forced smile does not reach the eyes. Alone, a forced smile can simply indicate that someone is trying to be polite. Always pay close attention when other deceptive movement clusters accompany a forced smile, as they can add additional proof that a person could be lying.

Smiles:

- **Tight smiles:** A tight, thin-lipped smile can indicate that someone is concealing information.

- **Closed mouth:** Genuine smiles are typically open. A closed smile, however, could be an effort to hide bad teeth.

- **Licking lips:** Lying can cause the mouth to dry out. People who lie are more likely to lick their lips after speaking.

Eye Contact

The eyes are called the "windows to the soul." The eyes continually communicate feelings. A person's eye contact can betray that he or she is being deceptive.

The Eyes:

- **Little to no eye contact:** A complete lack of eye contact may be an indication that someone is nervous and being deceptive, but it is not always an indication of lying. There could be cultural reasons for this behavior, so always be aware of any outside factors.

- **Looking to the left:** Moving the gaze to the left may indicate deception. It signals the imagination is being engaged. Left-handed individuals will shift their eyes to the right.

- **Unmoving eyes:** Some people who lie can look directly ahead without moving their eyes. They will not always shift their gaze or look away.

Changes in Posture

Posture can easily signal when a person is being deceptive. Lying will cause someone to focus more on his or her body language. This can cause people to exercise too much control or shift posture.

Posture:

- **Being still:** People who try to control their movements may be very still. Slight changes in positioning are normal. Abnormally still individuals may be hiding something.

- **Extreme changes:** Deception causes anxiety in most people. When body language changes from defensive positions to open, friendly postures. The clumsier these transitions increase the likelihood of deception.

- **Voice and movements do not correspond:** Body language typically reflects the voice and message of a speaker. When this is not the case, lying is indicated. For example, someone uses closed, defensive body language with a friendly tone and interaction.

Practical Illustration

Susan has to choose between two qualified candidates to run the new office for DEF Corporation. Both have the experience and skills necessary. Susan needs to give the job to someone she can trust because they will be working closely together. She knows from experience that it is possible for people to pass an interview with flying colors by being less than honest. She has regretted more than one hiring decision. To prepare, she brushed up on her body language.

In the first interview, she noted that the candidate looked forward without moving her eyes when asked about her relationships with her coworkers. Additionally, the tone of her voice did not match the closed body language. The second candidate matched her body language with her tone. She also had an open smile when answering questions about her past interpersonal relationships.

Chapter Nine:
Improve Your Body Language

Our bodies are apt to be our autobiographies.
Frank Gelett Burgess

People make snap judgments about each other based on body language. It is possible to improve your body language and the way that others view you. Give an air of confidence when meeting with colleagues and potential clients. Understanding the subtleties of body language makes it easier to improve your own. Simply pay attention to what you say and do.

Be Aware of Your Movements

It is important to be aware of your movements and what they mean. The best way to do this, however, is to make sure that the movements are genuine. Faked body language typically looks disjointed and unnatural. People can subconsciously pick up on these movements.

Tips:

- **Relax:** Try to relax and implement open body language. This will help prevent any nervous body signals.

- **Watch your hands:** Use comfortable gestures when talking. Do not hide your hands, and try to avoid fidgeting or touching your face.

- **Eye contact:** Maintain eye contact, but do stare at people.

- **Smile:** Avoid fake smiles. Give genuine smiles to instill trust.

- **Watch your head:** Look ahead; tilting is submissive. Nod occasionally to signal your interest.

The Power of Confidence

Improve body language by increasing personal confidence. Everyone has a personal level of confidence that is evident in body language. There are simple ways that can help improve confidence and body language.

Tips:

- **Exercise:** A strong body will boost personal confidence. It can also improve posture.

- **Dress:** Our appearance affects our confidence. Dressing well will help improve our self-esteem.

- **Posture:** An open posture will induce confidence. It will also improve the way others see you.

- **Speech:** Speak in a confident tone to increase your feelings of confidence. Do not mumble.

Position and Posture

Posture and body position are effective forms of communication. Pay attention to your position and posture and think about what they are communicating.

- **Posture:** Straight posture automatically increases confidence and alertness. Avoid slouching, but remain relaxed.

- **Position:** Open body positions communicate a relaxed and confident demeanor. Closed body positions indicate defensiveness.

Practice in a Mirror

Practice is the key to success. Many people have poor body mechanics. They do not realize the mechanics alter their posture or positions. Practicing body language in front of a mirror will give an accurate evaluation of what you are communicating.

What to Practice:

- **Note your posture:** Pay attention to any tendencies to slouch or hunch over. Practice your posture until it is correct.

- **Note your gestures:** Identify any nervous gestures you use, and consciously try to avoid them.

- **Practice talking:** Your tone should match your gestures and body language.

Practical Illustration

A CEO had difficulty with his public image. This caused the stock price to drop. His assistant suggested that he take the time to improve his body language. The CEO began exercising and taking the time to relax. In addition, he took the time to practice his body language in the mirror on a daily basis. As his posture and body language improved, so did his public image. People began to view him as a strong leader, and the stock price doubled the next year.

Chapter Ten:
Matching Your Words to Your Movement

...80% of what you understand in a conversation is
read through the body, not the words.
Deborah Bull

The key to instilling trust is matching body language to the words spoken. Movements will confirm or contradict what is said. Gestures will easily match what is said if the words reflect genuine feeling. Emotional awareness is necessary to communicate exactly what you mean. Unresolved emotions can affect body language.

Involuntary Movements

We do not control our involuntary movements. Emotions can affect our breathing, posture, gestures, and micro-expressions. People subconsciously pick up on involuntary movements, particularly when they contradict what is said. For example, increased respiration can indicate stress or anxiety. When practicing body language, be aware of involuntary movements. Reducing stress and finding healthy ways to express emotion will help limit involuntary movements.

Ways to reduce stress:

- Exercise

- Meditation

- Sufficient sleep

- Journaling

- Healthy diet

Say What You Mean

Deception is often part of polite communication. This will affect body language and movement. Communication is much more effective when you say what you mean. You should always practice being respectful and honest in your speech.

Honest Communication:

- **Be specific:** Stick to the facts when communicating. Do not rely on your emotions.

- **Self-edit:** Choose language that is not confrontational.

- **Have a goal:** Know the point of your communication, and do not ramble.

Always Be Consistent

Dependable communication creates trust. The key is to be consistently honest and open when communicating with others. Here are a few tips that will improve your communication style and increase consistency.

- **Speak plainly**: Avoid complex terms, and define any new terms used.

- **Listen:** Invite feedback and clarify information when necessary.

- **Adapt:** Pay attention to the body language and tone of others, and respond appropriately.

- **Be open:** Be open and honest in what is said and in your body language.

Actions Will Trump Words

People pay more attention to actions than words. We typically make decisions about someone within four seconds of a meeting. This is largely based on body language and behavior. If your body language is hostile, it does not matter how kind your words or tone are. Be aware of what your actions and gestures are communicating to those around you. Practice your body language skills and decode the body language of others:

What People Decide?

- Intelligence

- Trustworthiness

- Likability

- Decision to buy

Practical Illustration

Steve had a busy schedule, and he was under a great deal of stress. Rather than helping his sales, the extra work was hindering them. His sales dropped five percent over three months. His body language was affected by the stress on his system. A colleague advised Steve to make stress reduction a priority. Steve made a healthy lifestyle a priority. After eating well, exercising, and taking time to sleep, Steve's confidence and body language improved. He was more influential with new clients, and his sales increased by 15 percent six months later.

Closing Thoughts

- **Terry Galloway:** Deafness has left me acutely aware of both the duplicity that language is capable of and the many expressions the body cannot hide.

- **Dale Carnegie:** There are four ways, and only four ways, in which we have contact with the world. We are evaluated and classified by these four contacts: what we do, how we look, what we say, and how we say it.

- **Ralph Waldo Emerson:** When the eyes say one thing, and the tongue another, a practiced man relies on the language of the first.

- **Dee Hock:** If you don't understand that you work for your mislabeled subordinates, then you know nothing of leadership. You know only tyranny.

Special Invitation

Visioning and Goal Charting to Success

SUCCESS is yours with the right VISION and GOALS. With this report: develop unique vision; think strategically over the long term; take small, measurable action steps that guide you to your vision, eliminate distractions and be focused on your purpose

Visioning and Goal Charting to Success

http://www.divyaparekh.com/product/visioning-and-goal-charting-knowing-the-dream-living-the-expedition-and-reaching-the-destination/

Or

http://bit.ly/1iV4Blj

$50.00 value DISC (Personality Style) and Hidden Motivators Assessment - COMPLIMENTARY FOR THE READERS ONLY

Achieve PRODUCTIVITY, PERSONAL and FINANCIAL SUCCESS in your life by: Understanding yourself. You are invited to take a complimentary Hidden Motivators Profile assessment (invitation code: 44voyage) because understanding yourself will help you maximize PRODUCTIVITY, PERSONAL and FINANCIAL SUCCESS when your MOTIVATORS are at work.

http://dpgroup.abeo.us/voyage/

www.ingramcontent.com/pod-product-compliance
Lightning Source LLC
Chambersburg PA
CBHW021415170526
45164CB00002B/657

* 9 7 8 1 5 1 7 7 3 4 2 1 3 *